Plants

Flowers

Patricia Whitehouse

Heinemann Library
Chicago, Illinois

© 2002 Reed Educational & Professional Publishing
Published by Heinemann Library,
an imprint of Reed Educational & Professional Publishing,
Chicago, Illinois

Customer Service 888-454-2279
Visit our website at www.heinemannlibrary.com

Designed by Sue Emerson/Heinemann Library, Page layout by Carolee A. Biddle
Printed and bound in the U.S.A. by Lake Book

06 05 04 03 02
10 9 8 7 6 5 4 3 2 1

Library of Congress Cataloging-in-Publication Data
Whitehouse, Patricia, 1958-
    Flowers / Patricia Whitehouse.
        p. cm. — (Plants)
Includes index.
Summary: Introduces the physical characteristics, life cycle, and role
of flowers in the world of plants.
    ISBN 1-58810-520-2 (HC), 1-58810-729-9 (Pbk.)
    1. Flowers—Miscellanea—Juvenile literature. [1. Flowers.] I. Title.
II. Plants (Des Plaines, Ill.)
    QK49 .W52 2002
    582.13—dc21
                                        2001003649

Acknowledgments
The author and publishers are grateful to the following for permission to reproduce copyright material:
Title page, pp. 14, 23c E. R. Degginger Color Pic, Inc.; pp. 4, 8, 13L, 23g Nancy Rotenberg; pp. 5, 18 Dwight Kuhn; pp. 6, 23d, 23f Greg Ryan/Sally Beyer; pp. 7, 22, 23e, 24 David Derr; pp. 9, 23a Peter Smithers/Corbis; p. 10 Jay Ireland & Georgienne E. Bradley/Bradleyireland.com; p. 11 Michael Nichols/National Geographic Society; p. 12L Jane Burton/ Bruce Coleman Inc.; p. 12R Arthur R. Hill/Visuals Unlimited; p.13R Ed Reschke; p. 15 Cheryl Hogue/Visuals Unlimited; p.16 Winston Fraser; p. 17 Joy Spurr/Bruce Coleman Inc.; p. 19 Rick Wetherbee; pp. 20, 23b Joe McDonald/McDonald Wildlife Photography; p. 21 D. Cadagnaro/Visuals Unlimited

Cover photograph courtesy of Nancy Rotenberg

Every effort has been made to contact copyright holders of any material reproduced in this book.
Any omissions will be rectified in subsequent printings if notice is given to the publisher.

Special thanks to our advisory panel for their help in the preparation of this book:

Eileen Day, Preschool Teacher
Chicago, IL

Paula Fischer, K–1 Teacher
Indianapolis, IN

Sandra Gilbert,
Library Media Specialist
Houston, TX

Angela Leeper,
Educational Consultant
North Carolina Department
of Public Instruction
Raleigh, NC

Pam McDonald, Reading Teacher
Winter Springs, FL

Melinda Murphy,
Library Media Specialist
Houston, TX

Helen Rosenberg, MLS
Chicago, IL

Anna Marie Varakin,
Reading Instructor
Western Maryland College

The publishers would also like to thank Anita Portugal, a master gardener at the Chicago Botanic Garden, for her help in reviewing the contents of this book for accuracy.

Some words are shown in bold, **like this**.
You can find them in the picture glossary on page 23.

Contents

What Are Flowers?

stem

Flowers are a part of some plants.

They grow on the ends of branches or **stems.**

Flowers grow on trees, too.

These are an oak tree's flowers.

Why Do Plants Have Flowers?

pollen

stamen

Flowers make seeds.

First, a yellow dust called **pollen** forms on the **stamens.**

pistil

Next, the pollen drops into the **pistil**.

Then, seeds start to grow.

Where Do Flowers Come From?

Flowers come from **buds.**

Sun shines on the bud.

petals

bud

When the bud gets enough sunlight, it opens.

Then you can see the flower and its colorful **petals**.

How Big
Are Flowers?

orchid

Flowers are many sizes.

This orchid is smaller than a coin.

Some flowers are very big.

This one is almost as big as a man.

How Many Flowers Can Plants Have?

Some plants have one flower.

Some have more.

A sunflower looks like one flower, but it's not.

Each yellow part is one flower!

What Shapes Are Flowers?

Flowers have many shapes.

But flowers on one plant have the same shape.

Some flowers are round.

These flowers look like birds.

What Do Flowers Smell Like?

Many flowers smell like perfume.

But these flowers smell like skunks!

They are called skunk cabbage.

How Do People Use Flowers?

People use some flowers for food.

When you eat broccoli, you are eating flowers.

People use some flowers to make perfume.

People give flowers as presents.

How Do Animals Use Flowers?

Birds and bugs use flowers for food.

They drink a juice called **nectar** from the flower.

Some bugs hide inside flowers.

They can hide there because their color matches the flower.

Quiz

What parts of this flower do you remember?

Look for the answers on page 24.

? **?**

? **?**

Picture Glossary

bud
pages 8, 9

pistil
page 7

nectar
page 20

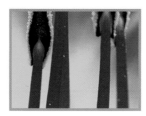
stamen
page 6

petal
page 9

stem
page 4

pollen
pages 6, 7

Note to Parents and Teachers

Reading for information is an important part of a child's literacy development. Learning begins with a question about something. Help children think of themselves as investigators and researchers by encouraging their questions about the world around them. Each chapter in this book begins with a question. Read the question together. Look at the pictures. Talk about what you think the answer might be. Then read the text to find out if your predictions were correct. Think of other questions you could ask about the topic, and discuss where you might find the answers. Assist children in using the picture glossary and the index to practice new vocabulary and research skills.

Index

Answers to quiz on page 22

petals | stamen

pistil | stem